D1327952

Germaine Greer was born in Melbourne and educated in Australia and at Cambridge University. Her first book, *The Female Eunuch*, (1969) remains one of the most influential texts of the feminist movement. Greer has had a distinguished academic career in Britain and the United States. She makes regular appearances in print and other media as a broadcaster, journalist, columnist and reviewer. Since 2001 she has been involved in rehabilitating sixty hectares of subtropical rainforest in south-east Queensland, Australia; in 2011, she set up Friends of Gondwana Rainforest, a UK charity, to help in financing that and similar projects.

Little Books on Big Ideas

GERMAINE GREER ON RAPE

BLOOMSBURY PUBLISHING

LONDON · OXFORD · NEW YORK · NEW DELHI · SYDNEY

BLOOMSBURY PUBLISHING
Bloomsbury Publishing Plc
50 Bedford Square, London, WC1B 3DP, UK

BLOOMSBURY, BLOOMSBURY PUBLISHING and the Diana logo are
trademarks of Bloomsbury Publishing Plc

First published in 2018 in Australia by Melbourne University Press,
an imprint of Melbourne University Publishing Limited
First published in Great Britain 2018

A catalogue record for this book is available from the British Library

ISBN: HB: 978-1-5266-0840-6; eBook: 978-1-5266-0839-0

2 4 6 8 10 9 7 5 3 1

Text design by Alice Graphics
Typeset by Typeskill
Printed and bound in Great Britain by CPI Group (UK) Ltd, Croydon CR0 4YY

To find out more about our authors and books visit
www.bloomsbury.com and sign up for our newsletters

What is rape?

The word 'rape' as used in this essay will apply only to penetration of the vagina of an unwilling human female by the penis of a human male. It will not be a portmanteau word into which are tipped sexual assaults of many kinds, involving outrages inflicted with different instruments in different parts of the body. In the interests of clarity, the category of rape has here been decluttered, and the instrument involved limited to the penis and the site of the penetration to the vagina.

Though some of us might like to think of the vagina as sacred, and casual use of it as a desecration, it has never been revered. The name 'vagina' is itself an insult. In Latin the word means 'scabbard', that is, 'sword sheath'. Why this ugly word should have been accepted by the 'civilised' world as the correct appellation for the birth canal is bewildering. The vernacular names for the vagina are now amongst the most shocking words anyone can say. Every English town used to have a Gropecunt Lane; now you won't find one anywhere.

These days the vagina is routinely accessed not only by the penis, but by a range of other instruments, to take cervical smears, swabs and samples for the diagnosis of a range of infections, for pregnancy terminations, for bimanual pelvic examinations, and for certain forms of ultrasound investigation. Today's women can expect to spend more time in the stirrups with a speculum in situ than any women in history. Not so long ago the vagina was feared as the entrance to the wild womb, but those days are long gone. Steroids have neutralised it. Even so, the vagina is not a hole like any other.

Rape is an awkward word, encumbered with all kinds of historical baggage, but its substitution by the expression 'sexual assault', as is the case with the penal code of New South Wales for example, is not an improvement. It has the effect of emphasising the level of violence involved, when rape itself need involve no violence at all. You can rape a sleeping woman without even waking her up.

Rape is not a rare and catastrophic event or an extraordinary act carried out by monsters; from the banal to the bestial rape is part of the tissue of everyday life. The US Rape,

Abuse and Incest National Network is wrong in describing rape as 'caused by the conscious decisions of a small percentage of the community to commit a violent crime'.[1] It is simply not true that 'All rapists are cowards, criminals, and losers and belong in prison' as Suicide.org founder Kevin Caruso tells us on the website. Nor is Professor John EB Myers of the McGeorge School of Law at the University of the Pacific right when he asserts that 'Nonconsensual sex without force is not rape'.[2]

As Margaret Sanger wrote in 1920, 'Woman was and is condemned to a system under which the lawful rapes exceed the unlawful ones a million to one'.[3] Bertrand Russell was thinking along the same lines when he pointed out that 'marriage is for women the commonest mode of livelihood, and the total amount of undesired sex endured by women is probably greater in marriage than in prostitution'.[4]

Rape is a jagged outcrop in the vast monotonous landscape of bad sex; we can only understand its prevalence and our inability to deal with it if we position it correctly within the psychopathology of daily life. Many years ago when I was a guest at a country house party, I was awoken in the wee small hours by the woman in the bedroom next door shouting at her husband. 'Rupert! Leave me alone. Stop it. Get off me.' The protests went on. At one point someone fell out of bed. The cries subsided, to be replaced by rhythmic creaking of bedsprings. Not long ago I asked her if she remembered the occasion. It turned out that it happened like that fairly often. Her husband slept badly, would read for half the night as she slept beside him, and would wake her up for sex that she didn't want. Fearful of waking the whole house, she would eventually stop struggling and protesting and give in.

'Was that rape?' she asked.

I replied that I was afraid it probably was, and added, 'But you wouldn't want him put away for seven years, would you?'

She laughed wryly. With five children between them, and a loving if stormy relationship, she certainly did not. A different kind of feminist might have set about persuading her that she should feel resentful of this treatment and take some sort of action to discourage her husband's casual use of her body, but I could see no merit in persuading her that her situation was oppressive or that rebellion—or separation—would be a better option. She has survived and they are still together, and have a dozen grandchildren.

If you google 'too tired for sex', say, you will read many accounts of non-consensual sex, some of them heartbreaking. It hurts to read the testimony of a woman with chronic pain who feels that it is her duty to pretend to enjoy sex with her husband, or the bitter words of the man whose wife winces if he touches her. How have we come to this pass? Non-consensual sex is banal and deeply ordinary but that is not to say that it is not an evil, with damaging consequences for both parties. A man who has sex with an unwilling woman alienates himself from intimacy with her. The woman who endures sex without pleasure suffers a steady corrosion of her self-esteem. Diurnal rape stifles love and imposes loneliness and withdrawal. The bitterest irony is that it is the unresponsive woman who will be blamed for the obliteration of what was once a mutual love.

In the 1970s when we still believed in sexual liberation, feminist reformers concerned themselves greatly with the female orgasm.[5] Nowadays, we have become resigned to the virtual certainty that a sizable proportion of the female population regularly fakes it. A random-sample telephone poll of 1501 Americans in 2004 showed that 48 per cent of women and 11 per cent of men faked orgasm.[6] A survey in the *Huffington Post* of 29 July 2012 found that 26 per cent of women fake orgasm every time they have sex. Another study carried out by British condom manufacturer Durex in 2017 arrived at the startlingly round figure of 'up to' 100,000,000 orgasms faked in Britain per week.[7] What faking it means is that, when we should be most intimate and most open with each other, communication is blocked by an intractable lie. Once you start faking it you have to go on.

Most discussions of rape concern themselves with cases of rape that were prosecuted. These represent a tiny proportion of the nonconsensual sex that actually occurs, almost none of which is ever reported; most of what is reported doesn't result in a prosecution, and most of the prosecutions don't result in convictions. Half-hearted attempts to deal with the shockingly high incidence of rape on college campuses have led to deeper confusion and bitterer antagonism between the sexes. Some of the hazing that was rife in Australian university colleges has been identified and exposed but the mindset that spawns it has not been eliminated. Instead it exists to harass and intimidate anti-rape activists by compiling 'pro-rape anti-consent' Facebook groups that glory in base misogyny.

Creating confusion

In the 1970s and 1980s attempts were made in all developed countries to reform rape laws, to give victims of sexual violence a better possibility of redress. Proof of resistance would no longer be required, the previous sexual history of the complainant could not be produced in evidence, and rape would be possible within marriage. Gender-neutral language was introduced for both victim and perpetrator and the definition of rape was widened to include penetration of mouth and anus as well as vagina. The results are contradiction and confusion.

Every jurisdiction in Australia has its own legislation for sexual offences. In South

Australia, Tasmania and Victoria, rape is called rape. In Queensland it can be called rape or sexual assault. In New South Wales it is sexual assault and in the Australian Capital Territory and the Northern Territory it is called 'sexual intercourse without consent'. In New Zealand it is called 'sexual viola-tion'. In South Australia and Queensland the maximum penalty is life, in the Northern Territory seventeen years, in New South Wales fourteen years and elsewhere various. In fact convictions in rape cases are rare, the maximum sentence is rarely imposed and the full sentence is rarely served out. While heinous stranger rape involving horrible injuries is assumed to lurk around every cor-ner, the reality is less spectacular, common, unapologetic and entirely unavenged.

Once upon a time everyone knew what rape was; it was the stealing of a woman from the man or men who owned her. What the raptors did with the women included taking them as slaves or concubines, selling them into slavery or marrying them. In all cases the woman was denied agency. Her captivity robbed her of honour, caste, dignity and prestige. To escape and make her way back to her family would as like as not result in her death because she was considered defiled. During millennia of tribal warfare, the possessions of the defeated, their wealth, their cattle, their slaves and their womenfolk, were the spoils of victory. Captive women walked behind the victor's car, along with prisoners of war, captured armaments and other members of the loser's household.

In 2012 British politician George Galloway was loudly condemned for expressing the opinion that what Julian Assange was accused of doing in the cases of Miss A and Miss W in Stockholm in 2010 did not constitute rape.

Woman A met Julian Assange, invited him back to her flat, gave him dinner, went to bed with him, had consensual sex with him, claims that she woke up to him having sex with her again. This is something which can happen, you know. I mean, not everybody needs to be asked prior to each insertion ...

It might be really bad manners not to have tapped her on the shoulder and said: 'Do you mind if I do it again?' It might be really sordid and bad sexual etiquette, but whatever else it is, it is not rape or you bankrupt the term rape of all meaning.[8]

In Galloway's universe the person who 'does it' is the male, and all that is required from the female is that she doesn't mind. Well might she reply, 'Please yourself.' The story of Assange's sexual misadventures reveals a good deal of similar misunderstanding about the ethics of heterosex, on the part not only of the perpetrator and the women complainants, but also of the judiciary, and this in Sweden, the country that has made the greatest effort to understand the true nature and extent of rape.

The complainants against Assange were two, Miss A and Miss W. Miss A said that he became violent in the course of a consensual exchange, refused to stop when she asked him and then penetrated her without a condom. Despite George Galloway, these two liberties are rape. The second complainant, Miss W, took Assange to her flat in Enköping intending to have sex with him, but once in bed he refused to wear a condom and she moved away from him. They had sex later in the night and Assange agreed to wear a condom, but the next morning she awoke to find him having unprotected sex with her. This was double rape.

Miss A and Miss W later made contact and joined forces in trying to get Assange to take a Sexually Transmitted Disease test. He refused, so both women went to the police only to learn that the police couldn't simply secure an order to make him take a test but would have to pass the women's allegations on to the prosecutor. The next day, 21 August, the case was transferred to Chief Public Prosecutor Eva Finne. On the following day, in answer to questions surrounding the incidents, Finne declared, 'I don't think there is reason to suspect that he has committed rape.' Notwithstanding, on 18 November 2010, Director of Public Prosecutions Marianne Ny ordered the detention of Julian Assange on suspicion of rape, three cases of sexual molestation and unlawful coercion. The Stockholm District Court acceded to the order and issued a European Arrest Warrant to execute it, but there was still disagreement. The warrant was appealed to the Svea Court of Appeal, which upheld its issuance but lowered the charge to suspicion of rape of a lesser degree, unlawful coercion and two cases of sexual molestation rather than three.

The sentence for rape in Sweden is imprisonment for not less than four and not more than ten years. The definition of rape under Swedish law is one of the broadest in the world, with the result that in 1996 Sweden registered almost three times the average number of rape offences as any of thirty-five other European countries. We will never know what punishments Assange's offences would have incurred; in 2015 one set of allegations against him was dropped, and in 2017 the other. Much could have been learned if he had actually faced trial, but his supporters genuinely believed that he was in danger of being extradited to the United States to face unrelated charges carrying a possible death sentence, and so he sought sanctuary in the Ecuadorian embassy in London, where he is to this day. When the decision to drop the second lot of charges was reported, Assange's Swedish lawyer, Per Samuelsson, declared it one of the happiest days of his legal career. 'This is obviously about consensual sex between two adults,' he declared, which just goes to show that the Swedish position on rape is no clearer than mud.[9]

The conundrum of consent

What distinguishes the crime of rape from other assaults is the insoluble conundrum of consent. Bianca Fileborn puts the case depressingly clearly:

> It is not enough for the complainant to know in themselves that they do not consent—the defendant must have knowledge of this non-consent to be considered legally guilty.[10]

The issue was brought home to the Australian public by the trial, conviction, and eventual acquittal of Luke Lazarus of the crime of anal rape. In May 2013 eighteen-year-old Saxon Mullins travelled with her best friend to Sydney from her home on the Central Coast for a night out. On the dancefloor of a nightclub part-owned by his father, she met Luke Lazarus and danced with him. According to her account, he said he would take her to a VIP area but took her into a back lane instead. He pulled her stockings and underwear down. She pulled them back up and asked to return to her friend. He said (as she related in a *Four Corners* programme in which she gave up her anonymity in May 2018), 'Put your fucking hands on the wall.' Lazarus then tried to penetrate her anally but failed, so he told her to get down on all fours and arch her back. She complied and the rape was completed.

Mullins was left hysterical and bleeding. When she got to her sister's house, where she had arranged to stay, her sister insisted that she go to the police. Next day Dr Ellie Freedman, director of the Northern Sydney Sexual Assault Service, found it difficult to examine Mullins because she was so sore. Lazarus was charged, tried in 2015, convicted and sentenced to a minimum of three years' jail. An appeal was brought on the grounds that the verdict was not reasonable. A judge-only retrial was ordered. Judge Robyn Tupman accepted that while Mullins believed that she wasn't consenting, Lazarus did believe that she was consenting, and acquitted him. In doing so she made an error by taking into account the defendant's self-intoxication, which is not to be considered in mitigation under New South Wales law. Even so, a Crown appeal against the acquittal was dismissed in November 2017 and Tupman's verdict upheld.

Historian Hiram Kümper dates the emergence of consent as the defining issue in rape surprisingly early:

> … from the twelfth century onwards the crime was recognized as a sexual offence with the lack of the woman's consent as its core element … this new consensual perspective on the constitution of the deed, brought about new juridical problems. Once an inner disposition is in question—and the consenting will or its absence is truly an inner disposition—methods and instruments are needed to discern reliably such an inner state of mind. This becomes,

and still is, the central problem of assessing rape in the courtroom.[11]

Consent is explained in different ways in different jurisdictions. Consent and what can be interpreted as a sign of consent or lack of it cannot be so defined. The jury consults its own understanding of the events as presented to them. Mullins had ten standard drinks before she turned up at Soho at 4 a.m.; she danced with Lazarus; she accompanied him outside; she complied with his instructions. Even so the jury found him guilty; it was the female judge who acquitted him. When the law insists that while there is the smallest possibility that the perpetrator genuinely believed that his victim consented to her humiliation, he must be cleared of all charges, assailants will be reassured that they are practically certain to get away with rape.

There is now a presumption that the issue of consent is not problematical. Campaigners chant, 'No means no and yes means yes' and 'Consent is not the absence of no but the presence of yes', and so forth, as if sexual interaction was a matter of signing on a dotted line. Some universities in the United States are asking individuals intending to have sex to set out the conditions under which they are prepared to go ahead, specifying condom use, orifices accessible, ejaculation where, as if sex could be programmed in advance. According to a meta-analysis published in 2015, as many as 60 per cent of rape survivors don't acknowledge that they were raped even to themselves.[12] US TV star Gabrielle Union, who was raped at gunpoint in 1992, says now, 'Regardless of what I *think* may have happened that night twenty-five years ago, after reading all 700 pages of the trial transcript, I still don't actually *know*. Nor does anyone who was not in that room.'[13]

Let us take a simple example of the complexity of consent. Ella is a single mother, living with her daughter in a little A-frame house in woodland. She has had a brief relationship with one of her co-workers which she has decided to end. Her four-year-old daughter is asleep in the apex of the A-frame and Ella is watching TV when the ex-boyfriend comes knocking. He refuses to go away and keeps shouting and knocking. She lets him in, hoping to convince him that she is no longer interested so that he goes away without more ado. He grabs her and forces himself upon her. If she fights him the noise will awaken her daughter. The thought of her little girl's shock and terror is too much. She gives in. In fact his aim was not to revive the relationship but to humiliate and degrade her. At work next day he derided her in front of her workmates. Soon after she gave up her job and left the district.

Even Ella was not sure that giving in was not consent. She didn't think she had been raped. If a woman herself does not know whether she is consenting or giving in, a man certainly cannot know. It is quite unfair to allow him the right to decide the issue. There is no objective sign of consent on the one hand or withdrawal of consent on the other. The burden of proof required to prove rape in a criminal court can never be satisfied; if we are to abandon the formulation used in many jurisdictions, that the defendant who reasonably believed that the victim consented is innocent, and rely instead upon the victim's statement that she did not consent as sufficient, then we will have to lighten the tariff. We will have to reduce the penalties for rape. The mere suggestion will cause an outcry which is one good reason for making it.

Sex as a bloodsport

Twenty years ago when I was teaching at Warwick University and observing first hand the effects of sexual depredations on my female students, it became clear to me that the perpetrators of sexual harassment were not a typical sample of the male members of the university community but rather a self-selecting group of serial offenders. I suggested that we set up a database where women could both record their experiences and investigate whether a man they were seeing or thinking of seeing had abused other women. The reaction was horror. What if what was alleged was untrue? I had no idea how to go about designing such a database and the only people I knew to ask were all men. I put forward the idea occasionally but nobody came forward. I stopped talking about it and eventually I stopped thinking about it.

In 2014 four names of 'sexual assault violators on campus' appeared on the wall of a women's washroom at Columbia University, each in a different handwriting. At Brown University appeared another list, this time of five names, with the heading 'Brown Survivors Speak'. Women were beginning to 'kick ass and take names, talk loud and draw a crowd', but there was no way the universities could capitulate. The unproven allegations were actionable, the inscribing of them vandalism. The graffiti were cleaned off; no further action was taken.

At Yale female students have recently been using anonymous Google docs to list the names of sexual predators on campus. In 2017 an anonymous open-sourced list of 'Shitty Media Men' appeared online; within twelve hours, seventy men in the New York media world had been named as sexual predators. The outcry was immediate. The author, journalist Moira Donovan, found herself vilified and threatened. She had intended to give women a safe place to report sexual harassment and abuse, but there can be no such place. The information about the dangerous men was anonymous and the potential effects of such information devastating, not least for Donovan who lost her job.[14] Within twenty-four hours the list was taken down but the reverberations continue.

What was needed was a secure way of providing information from survivors of sexual harassment and assault that would inform the authorities of real and present danger in their communities. The Dear Colleague Letter issued by the Obama administration in 2011 in an attempt to check the rate of sexual assault on American campuses (unchanged at 20 per cent since the 1980s) had placed college authorities under an obligation to investigate all complaints of sexual abuse without giving them the means of conducting such investigations in a way that would protect them from litigation. The current US Secretary of Education, Betsy DeVos, has since replaced the 2011 Dear College Letter before it could be declared unconstitutional.

Meanwhile Jessica Ladd had found a better way. She was studying for a postgraduate degree in infectious disease epidemiology at Johns Hopkins University when she became involved in a programme called Sexual Health. She is also a survivor of sexual assault. When, more than a year after the event, she finally plucked up the courage to report her assault to the college authorities she found the process as traumatising as the assault. Years later, she realised that technology could supply a means of healing the victim, by providing a safe place for her to describe her experience. Users of the website she set up can record their experience in a time-stamped document, which is secure and encrypted so that even the operators of the website cannot read it. It is then kept as it were in escrow to be sent to the school only if the content of the document matches with another account. In 2015 the system was piloted at Claremont College and the University of San Francisco. Reports of sexual assault quadrupled. In 2016 Sexual Health Innovations was renamed Callisto. At the time of writing thirteen educational institutions have signed on.

Analysis of the data shows, not only that 15 per cent of sexual assault survivors who opted into the matching system had been assaulted by the same perpetrator as another survivor in the system, but that 90 per cent of assaults are committed by repeat offenders, who perpetrate an average of six assaults each. 'The strongest predictor of future sexual violence is past sexual violence'. This information is important and enforcers of the law should be made aware of it. One kind of cold, calculating sexual predator is a recidivist, will offend again and his attacks will become ever more cruel. When users of Callisto are asked why they have been moved to submit a report, they usually reply that it is to protect others. How crucial that is can be gauged from the following example.

In 2002 a student at Jerry Falwell's Liberty University in Lynchburg, VA, made a complaint of rape, naming college footballer Jesse Matthew as her assailant. Investigation came to an end when she withdrew her complaint. Soon after Matthew left Liberty and went to play football at Christopher Newport University in Newport News, where he was accused of rape again. Again the complaint was withdrawn. A month later Matthew quit the football team, and a month after that he left the university. In 2005 he was found guilty of a brutal attack on a woman and jailed for three life terms. In March 2016 faced with DNA evidence from the earlier trial, Matthew pleaded guilty to the first-degree murders of Morgan Harrington in 2009 and Hannah Graham in 2014. If the women who complained in 2002 and 2003 had stuck to their guns these two women might still be alive. If Callisto had been around in 2002 and 2003 Matthew might have been identified as an extremely dangerous predator. The total number of his victims is not yet known. The name given to the abandonment of so many rape cases because the survivors cannot face the court process is 'attrition'. Attrition is yet another reason why police are reluctant to invest scarce resources in investigating rape.

Callisto has its critics. Colleges and universities that have signed on are bypassing the criminal justice system and taking it upon themselves to apportion blame, with no evidence beyond the accusations made by survivors. As one online commentator (alundra 3434) wrote in response to an online video of Jessica Ladd speaking on the talk-show *Late Night with Seth Meyers*:

> So, all I need is a friend and together we can throw another person under the bus via the anonymity of the internet. Sounds absolutely foolproof.

In November 2017 entrepreneur Sakshi Thakur won a cash prize from the Wade Institute of Entrepreneurship at Melbourne

University for setting up a sexual harassment reporting platform called Skip Labs, which appears to resemble Callisto except that it is directed towards employers rather than teaching institutions. The idea is that the software package can collect information from 'de-identified' complainants and guide organisations 'through research-backed processes and actions, resulting in positive outcomes'.[15] This, it must be said, will not be easy and may actually prove impossible.

Victim or exhibit?

The rule used to be that a woman alleging rape had to resist to her utmost. If she ceased to resist before the assault was completed, she would be deemed to have consented. Resistance would contribute to proof of non-consent, but there had to be evidence of it in the way of injuries. The demand for evidence of utmost resistance was mitigated in the 1940s in America at least to evidence of 'reasonable' resistance, which held on in some states until 2017. In Australia the condition of the complainant may be a factor that is taken into account by the public prosecutor in considering whether or not to bring the matter to trial. In many jurisdictions rape victims can apply for compensation, which is usually expressed in terms of money, but they must be able to show evidence of injury.

At trial evidence of resistance is no longer demanded, but juries are only human. Evidence of the victim's struggle helps them to resolve their uncertainty about whether or not there was consent. As long as they are uncertain they cannot find the accused guilty. Researchers at the School of Social Work at the University of Nebraska divided resistance into five kinds in ascending order of effectiveness, beginning with no resistance, followed by non-forceful verbal resistance (pleading, crying and/or assertively refusing), then forceful verbal resistance (screaming and/or yelling), then physical resistance (wrestling,

struggling, pushing, striking, biting and/
or using a weapon), then fleeing (running,
walking away, and/or fleeing in a car).[16] To
anyone familiar with everyday rape, the above
scenarios all seem far-fetched. The situations
adumbrated are hard to reconcile with everyday rape. And we might suspect that most of
the situations referred to were examples
of that rarest of rapes, stranger rape.

If a man punches you in the eye, you are
not expected to have pleaded with him not
to for the crime to be accepted as an assault.
If you are sitting at your cash register and
someone demands the cash in it, you will
not be accused of consent if you simply hand
it over. Only in the prosecution of rape is
evidence of resistance an issue. A startling
Swedish study, published in the journal

Acta Obstetricia et Gynecologica Scandinavica in May 2018, shows just how 'normal' it is for victims of sexual assault to experience a temporary paralysis that keeps them from fighting back or screaming. The researchers spoke to nearly 300 women who went to an emergency clinic in Stockholm within one month of a rape or attempted rape. Seventy per cent of the women said they experienced significant 'tonic immobility', or involuntary paralysis, during the attack.

A woman who accuses a man of rape is not a plaintiff, still less a prosecutor. The accused has civil rights that cannot be abrogated. He cannot be made to incriminate himself; he need not speak at all and does not have to endure cross-examination, and he has the right to see his accuser. He is entitled to counsel, and if he cannot afford it the state must supply it. These considerations apply in most jurisdictions that inherited British common law, including Australian ones. Because men accused of rape are so often cleared, there is a strong movement nowadays for the extension of anonymity to the accused as well as the accuser in rape cases. In Britain this has already been tried. In 1976 the Labour Government introduced anonymity for both parties in rape trials, but in 1988, as a consequence of the obstacles that it placed in the way of police investigations, the anonymity provision was removed.

A woman who chooses to report her rape to the police becomes evidence. In 2016 a young Australian woman who had been drugged and raped by a colleague on a night out with friends two years before told her story to the ABC. We shall call her Belle. Belle complained to the police, and became a piece of evidence. She went to hospital to be probed, swabbed, and questioned. The rape kit thus assembled is supposed to be kept in case the complainant wishes to make a formal complaint, whereupon it will be analysed and the results communicated to the police. Otherwise the kit will be kept for up to a year and then destroyed. There is a cost involved in working up the forensic report; in some cases the complainant will be expected to meet that cost, especially if she withdraws her complaint. The *New Daily* has identified 6741 untested kits in New South Wales, Victoria and Queensland, and minimal or no tracking of kits in South Australia, the Australian

Capital Territory and the Northern Territory. Given how many sex predators are repeat offenders, identifying and recording DNA in every case would be a significant way of protecting the public. Recent coordinated testing in Detroit, Memphis and Cleveland identified 1300 repeat offenders.

In Belle's case the police and medical staff were professional and concerned, but by the time she had endured the full array of testing and repeated extended bouts of questioning, she was exhausted. Committal hearings followed in the local court, where it was decided on whether to proceed. In New South Wales 38 per cent of cases will be withdrawn at this level, 72 per cent of them before the indictment is even filed. The accused was eventually arrested and released on bail. The trial was scheduled and cancelled several times, as the people in Belle's male-dominated workplace let it be known that they offered neither sympathy nor support. The chances of a conviction were never good. Even with a conviction the penalty might be nothing more than a good behaviour bond. Currently, the average custodial sentence for sexual assault in New South Wales is thirty-four months. In court Belle was cross-questioned for five hours. The assailant remained silent. The jury declared him not guilty.

The raped woman's ordeal grows steadily worse. Joan Smith, chair of the Mayor of London's Violence against Women and Girls panel, and Claire Waxman, Victims Commissioner for London, recently tabled the following protest:

Complainants now face a complete loss of privacy, having to hand over their mobile phones, tablets and even work computers, containing a mass of personal material such as text messages, photographs and even medical records. Few people realise that even deleted material will be examined, including pictures that may have been taken while the victim was in an abusive relationship.[17]

Defendants meanwhile are not obliged or even expected to hand over their phones and computers in the event of a rape investigation. Detectives have to obtain consent from a superintendent to access even minimal electronic information about a suspect, such as the phone numbers he called just before and after an alleged attack. In the United States rape victims have been required to take polygraph tests. In 1996 according to ABC *Primetime* 200 clients at US rape crisis centres were threatened with arrest or charges of perjury if they failed them. Other kinds of lie detection, Voice Stress Analysis, Handwriting Analysis, and Statement Validity Analysis have also been used. Though the results are not admissible as evidence in court, lie detectors are still widely used in the work-up towards a trial.

There are now further problems caused by the way disclosure is being handled. With so much material stored on computers—it is estimated that the average smartphone contains data equivalent to around 30,000 A4 pages—British police say that the process of examining it could add a year or eighteen months to a rape investigation. In Australia too rape complainants can wait for years before the matter is dealt with. In 2016 Australian newspapers reported on the case of 'Amanda', who was abused by a family friend over six months at the age of fourteen; she confided in her sister at the age of twenty, and reported the matter to the police soon after. The case dragged on for six years. The perpetrator then pleaded guilty to five of the seven charges against him and agreed to serve ten months in jail. Amanda then brought a civil case against him when she was awarded $40,000 in damages.

Joystick or weapon?

Why are women so afraid of rape? If we stick to the kernel of the offence, it involves the most vulnerable part of a man's body, his penis. Most of men's pet names for their penises signify weakness and foolishness. Even basketballer Steven Adams refers to his famous equipment as 'junk'. More diffident men use pet names like 'willy' or 'winkle' or 'plonker' or 'todger'. Australians use 'dick' often in connection with 'head' to mean complete fool.

According to Patricia D Rozee's article 'Fear of Rape' in the *Women's Studies Encyclopedia*, women fear rape more than any other violent offence. This intense fear of rape, Rozee says, common amongst a significant majority of girls and women, develops in childhood, between the ages of two and twelve. She reports that women participating in the studies claim to remember hearing parental warnings about stranger danger at very young ages. In *The Female Fear: The Social Cost of Rape*, Margaret T Gordon and Stephanie Riger say that fully one-third of the women in their study reported worrying about rape once a month or more. Others said that the fear of rape is just something that lives in the back of their minds at all times, even when it wasn't present in conscious thought. Another third of the participants claimed to never worry about rape but even so they took precautions to guard against it.

In *Against Our Will: Men, Women and Rape*, her groundbreaking feminist work on rape, Susan Brownmiller famously wrote:

A world without rapists would be a world in which women moved freely without fear of men. That some men rape provides a sufficient threat to keep all women in a constant state of intimidation, forever conscious of the knowledge that the biological tool must be held in awe, for it may turn to weapon with sudden swiftness born of harmful intent.[18]

The 'biological tool' is the penis, presumably; to suppose that it turns into a weapon is to imagine that what does the harm in a rape is the poor old penis. To buy into such a notion is to share one of the male delusions about the penis, that it is an awesome, powerful thing. An elbow, a thumb even, can do you more harm than a penis. It is a nonsense for our daughters to be more frightened of penises than our sons are of knives or guns.

Can it be true that rape 'is nothing more or less than a conscious process of intimidation by which all men keep all women in a state of fear', as Brownmiller has it?[19] Irrational fears are not caused by the objects that are feared. It is not ghosts that make people afraid of ghosts or cats that make people afraid of cats. For Brownmiller to present the penis as capable of turning itself into a weapon is to present an irrational fear as a reasonable response to a present danger. Most of us are in greater danger of being mugged than raped, but we are not aware of mugging as an everpresent danger. If we were more aware of the danger of mugging we wouldn't be so mad keen to encumber ourselves with conspicuous handbags.

Women do fantasise about being raped. Researchers at Notre Dame and the University of North Texas gave standard psychological tests to 355 undergraduates, who they thought constituted a representative sample of young female Americans. Then the researchers surveyed the women's sexual fantasies. Among the 32 per cent of respondents who admitted fantasies of being forced by men, 33 per cent experienced them less than once a year, 26 per cent a few times a year, 20 per cent once a month, 11 per cent weekly, and 9 per cent at least four times a week.[20] The researchers did not interpret this as meaning that the young women harboured a desire to be raped, because in the fantasy they were in control of the scenario.

One of many misconceptions about rape held by women is that it is prompted by overwhelming sexual desire. Women do fantasise that they can inspire that kind of feeling in a man; every heavy breather on the telephone is pandering to a female delusion. We find it in chicklit (the largest-selling genre of fiction) whenever the hero groans in the grip of passion, 'God, I want you', 'You drive me crazy', or words to that effect.

In 1963 a pathologist working on the case of the Sydney mutilator told me that when he took out of their container a set of male genitalia recovered from the harbour, he found tattooed on the penis the words, 'a present for a good girl'. Men misperceive women's reactions during sex. Because their penis gives them so much pleasure, it is difficult for them to imagine that it is not doing anything for the recipient of their attentions. We are not surprised to find men expressing the opinion that women get pleasure from being raped. It is more depressing to find that more than a few contributions to online discussions purport to come from women who have enjoyed being raped, some of whom claim that the only time they have experienced orgasm was in the course of a rape.

Healing the victim

How much damage does the rapist do? As long as we are talking physical injuries, these are usually the consequence of the assault, not of the rape per se. Accounts of the psychological consequences of rape attribute the woman's suffering to the rape itself, which has the effect of making it sound catastrophic. Raped women will be told not only that they are irrevocably damaged in soul and body but that if they do not acknowledge this they are in denial. When we encounter a system in which women reporting rape are, besides providing sperm samples and blood tests and an extended narrative of events, to be examined by a psychiatrist and a diagnosis arrived at, we might wonder if they will ever be allowed to get over it. Getting over it becomes a suspect activity in itself.

In 1974 Ann Wolbert Burgess, founder of the rape crisis counselling service at Boston City Hospital, and Lynda Lytle Holmström of Boston College published their account of what they called Rape Trauma Syndrome in the *American Journal of Psychiatry*.[21]

They interviewed and followed up 146 patients admitted during a one-year period to the emergency ward of a city hospital who complained of having been raped. Using their analysis of the ninety-two adult women rape victims in the sample, they identified a rape trauma syndrome which came in three forms: a typical form, compounded reaction and silent reaction.

It seemed to more than one observer that the authors of the article in the *American Journal of Psychiatry* had assumed what they needed to prove.

Criticisms of the scientific validity of the RTS construct are that it is vague in important details; it is unclear what its boundary conditions are; it uses unclear terms that do not have a basis in psychological science; it fails to specify key quantitative relationships; it has not undergone subsequent scientific evaluation since the 1974 Burgess and Holmström study; there are theoretical allegiance effects; it has not achieved a consensus in the field; it is not falsifiable; it ignores possible mediators; it is not culturally sensitive; and it is not suitable for being used to infer that rape has or has not occurred.[22]

Ann Burgess is now principally known as the original of Wendy Carr in the *Mindhunter* TV series.

According to the US Rape, Abuse and Incest National Network 33 per cent of rape victims contemplate suicide and 13 per cent attempt it. A now famous victim impact statement from 2016 reads in part 'you [the assailant] took away my worth, my privacy, my energy, my time, my intimacy, my confidence, my own voice, until today'.[23] Why should a sexual assault take away these precious, intangible things? There is a clue to how to reclaim them in the last two words. The victim who takes over her narrative becomes a survivor.

Diagnosis of RTS gradually gave way before an identification of the distress caused by rape as a form of Post-Traumatic Stress Disorder. In the case of PTSD more rigorous assessment had been carried out and clear criteria had been established. Now we learn that whereas only 10 to 20 per cent of veterans will suffer PTSD, 70 per cent of rape victims will suffer moderate to severe distress, 'a larger percentage than for any other violent crime'. As usual we are here confronted with unanswerable questions. Most rape is not accompanied by physical injury or carried out by men unknown to the victim, nor is it followed by flashbacks or is it ever identified as a crime. In the case of a woman who chooses to report the event, we have no idea how much of her distress is caused by the work-up itself, by the compilation of the forensic evidence, by her having to tell her story over and over and in public and then to defend it both in the committal stage and later in the court-room. The most catastrophic shock must surely come when, as far too often happens, the jury does not convict. Nothing in the lit-erature of PTSD after rape deals with these experiences. For all the intellectual effort and energy that has gone into getting the law of rape to make sense, conviction rates are fall-ing. Meanwhile the true extent of non-con-sensual sex remains unimaginable.

Cure, kill or castrate the perp?

In 1982 the British Lord Chief Justice, Lord Lane, declared, 'Rape is always a serious crime. Other than in wholly exceptional circumstances, it calls for an immediate custodial sentence...'[24] His reasons were five, to mark the gravity of the offence, to emphasise public disapproval, to serve as a warning to others, to punish the offender, and to protect women. In the same document we read, 'sex without consent is readily acknowledged as being rape'. Heaven knows what Lane would have had to say about the suspended sentences given to one in ten of the men convicted of rape in the state of Victoria between 2011 and 2016. Given the reality, that non-consensual sex is possibly commoner than the consensual variety and that only a tiny proportion of it ever comes before the law and most of those prosecutions do not result in a conviction, Lane would appear to be living in cloud cuckoo land.

Penalties for rape are wildly inconsistent. In China, Afghanistan, the United Arab Emirates, Egypt, Bangladesh, Iran, Saudi Arabia, India, Pakistan and North Korea, the penalty can be death. In the United Emirates the rapist can face a firing squad; in Iran he can be hanged. There are those in the twittersphere who are happy to declare that they 'actually think rapists should be executed' because 'rape is the worst of all crimes; worse than murder…' Another recommended putting 'a bullet between their eyes'. Yet another recommended blinding a rapist to remove the source of temptation.

Given the admitted prevalence of sexual assault at about one in five women over a lifetime compared with the rarity of convictions, we have to wonder why rape sentences are so long. Lane believed that harsher sentences would encourage more raped women to come forward, but it is the savagery of the sentence that pushes juries toward extending the benefit of the doubt. No one has to my knowledge considered the possibility that harsher sentencing could persuade a man guilty of sexual assault that he might as well kill his victim, because his sentence is likely to be shorter for murder than it would have been for rape, with the added bonus that his victim could not give evidence against him.

The first husband of TV executive Vivian McGrath grabbed her round the throat and squeezed till she lost consciousness, then dragged her across the floor over glass from the lamps he had smashed. She came to when he was looking for something in the kitchen and ran for her life to the police station. She made a statement—'My husband tried to kill me'—and was taken to hospital. He was charged with assault; a restraining order was issued. When he was later convicted he was given a suspended sentence as a first-time offender.[25] If he'd raped her he'd have got five to ten years, first-time offender or no. How can that make sense?

Compare it with what happened to homeless illegal immigrant Ashraf Miah. In June

2017 Lillian Constantine was walking home in Ramsgate, England, in the dark because the streetlights had been turned off in an economy drive, when she was attacked by Miah. She had been lighting her way with her phone and turned on its camera. When Miah continued to wrestle with her even though she told him she was videoing him, she decided that he had to be 'an absolute maniac'. She reported the event to the police. In court Miah pleaded guilty to attempted rape and was convicted as well of 'sexual assault by penetration and sexual assault without penetration'. (If he actually understood the verdict he is a better man than I am.) He was sentenced to nine years in jail, plus four years on extended licence to be followed by deportation back to Bangladesh.

The idea of castrating convicted rapists has been around for years and never quite seems to go away. These days it is most often invoked as a way of controlling those guilty of the rape of children. In some cases the acceptance of chemical castration is made a condition of parole. In Britain the chief architect of the Ministry of Justice's ongoing programme of voluntary chemical castration is Professor Don Grubin; the drugs used are of two kinds, serotonin uptake inhibitors and anti-androgens—in use since 2007, their use is now to be massively expanded. Turkey, Argentina, Moldova, Poland, Portugal, Macedonia, Estonia, Israel, Australia, India and Russia all use chemical castration. In Western Australia and Victoria the drugs are administered by quarterly injection.

Meanwhile in the Czech Republic, ninety-four surgical castrations have been carried out between 2000 and 2012. Repeat sexual offenders in California have been known to ask for surgical castration as a way of avoiding indefinite incarceration. Contributors to online debates have suggested penectomy as well, with the proviso that 'the offender must be absolutely guilty without any shadow of doubt'. As if.

Just as it is not the penis that commits rape, and not testosterone that drives it and not overwhelming sexual desire either, castration whether surgical or chemical will not eliminate men's hatred of women. Rape is not a sex crime, but a hate crime. When the jock tells his adoring fan 'no kissing', turns her face down and penetrates her from behind, his aim is to leave her 'fucked' and good for nothing.

Damage limitation

Banal rape, the kind that happens when a man has sex with a woman without concerning himself that she is not into it and doesn't want it, is not something that anyone but the participants can prevent. Sex is at least as difficult as conversation; sex as a substitute for conversation doesn't compute. After eight years of marriage and three children together, Ivanka Trump and Jared Kushner are said to have weekly date nights, when they are a courting couple again. What that should mean is that they both talk to each other and both listen to each other. In fact Ivanka has said that Jared will spend most of the evening on his phone.

There is an alternative to a criminal prosecution and that is to bring a civil action for damages against the perpetrator. In such an event the raped individual is not merely a chunk of evidence that a crime may have been committed, but actively alleging harm and demanding redress. The burden of proof required is lower; the jury will decide on the 'balance of probability' whether or not the abuse actually happened. The criminal case frames the harm as between the perpetrator and the state; a civil case not only frames the harm as being done by the rapist to the victim, but can allege responsibility on the part of third parties on whose properties the rape took place. However, hiring a lawyer to pursue a claim for damages can be costly and there has to be evidence of damage. There is also the possibility that one of the parties involved will allege 'comparative fault' by way of making the victim partly responsible for the attack. There is no certainty either that costs will be awarded to the plaintiff. When 'Amanda' (for whom see p. 49) brought a civil action against the man who abused her and was awarded $40,000 in damages, half of it went to her lawyers.

In the case of NRL star Jarryd Hayne, the 25-year-old woman accusing him of rape has brought a civil case after prosecutors decided against initiating a criminal trial. In December 2015 when he was playing football with the San Francisco 49ers, Hayne met the complainant in a San Jose bar and travelled to his house with her. She claims that she was too drunk to have been capable of consent to what ensued and that therefore he raped her. The issue is complicated by the putative victim's claim that she was a virgin at the time and saving herself for marriage, and that she suffered vaginal pain for months before attending a hospital emergency department in April 2016 to be treated for acute pelvic floor pain. The hospital judged that she had suffered a sexual assault and reported the matter to the police as required by California law. In defence documents already filed by Hayne, he denied that she had suffered an injury and insisted that she 'willingly engaged in sexual interaction that did not include sexual intercourse'. Her civil lawsuit in the District Court alleges sexual battery and claims punitive damages. His lawyers have called for the case to be dismissed with prejudice and costs awarded to Hayne.

In similar cases huge damages have been awarded to the complainant. In 2001 Lisa Simpson, a sophomore at the University of Colorado, reported to police that she had been gang-raped by high school footballers in town for a recruiting weekend. Her attorney Baine Kerr then filed a civil rights lawsuit against the university under Title IX, arguing that the university fostered a culture around football that put women at risk. The case dragged on for nearly five years before the university settled with Simpson for $2.5 million. In 2009 Arizona State University agreed to pay $850,000 to another woman who had been raped by footballer Darnel Henderson, who had a documented history of attacking women on campus. The settlement also allowed for a women's safety officer and public disclosure of the amount paid in settlement. Unfortunately, though the successful litigants hoped that they had made the campus safer for women, ASU had three more Title IX complaints on file when in 2017 a fourth was added. Campus activists claim that of 3660 complaints of sexual misconduct, the university had acted on only sixty-two.

When it comes to what some people have dubbed 'simple rape', which involves only one perpetrator who is known to the adult victim, no weapons, no injuries, and no plying with drugs or alcohol, the kind which is virtually impossible to prove in a court of law, there are two possible courses of action, mediation and restoration.

Mediation does not require the perpetrator to admit the offence. It proceeds on the pattern of dispute resolution. She says he raped her; he says he didn't. He says she consented; she says she didn't. He says he thought she consented; she says he knew she didn't. The Obama Dear Colleague Letter that instructed American institutions in receipt of public funding that it was their duty to investigate and adjudicate rape complaints, specifically banned informal negotiation between the parties, apparently on the grounds that this would be traumatic for the complainant. When the complainant and the alleged perpetrator are members of the same community and will have spent time together before the alleged event and may expect to have to come into proximity with each other afterwards, it seems unlikely that coming face to face with each other will be shocking or terrifying.

Many a complainant regrets that she gets no chance to tell her story, nor does she ever receive an apology, which can go some way to appeasing her justified sense of outrage. In reality the management of mediation in rape cases turns out to be very difficult. The mediator needs to understand a complex set of issues and to have been trained in eliciting the truth as both parties see it.

Broadly speaking, the mediator will meet with the parties separately to get their side of the story. When they come face to face the mediator will insist on certain ground rules; both parties must listen to each other without interruption. The process would seem most suited to campus rape; in such a situation both parties are likely to be close in age, social standing and IQ. Post-conviction mediation with a possibility of reducing the sentence is an option. There is no evidence however that access to mediation improves the rate of reporting of rape, which has actually fallen in many places.

In April 2017 the Melbourne-based South Eastern Centre Against Sexual Assault announced that it was providing a 'world-first' platform for sexual abuse survivors to confront and communicate with perpetrators. The sessions were to take place outside the formal criminal justice process; conversations and details discussed during the mediation sessions could not be used to incriminate the alleged perpetrators. Alleged perpetrators had to accept and acknowledge some responsibility before meeting with the survivors. The Michael Kirby Centre for

Public Health and Human Rights at Monash University is now evaluating the programme. Carolyn Wort who headed the pilot programme has twenty years' experience in running similar informal programmes. What is more, anonymous reports supplying details of when and where the offences occurred and descriptions of the offenders will be circulated to police all over Australia. As we have seen, versions of this procedure have been tried and all have run into difficulties.

Restorative justice is an idea as various as the people it seeks to deal with. It can be a series of family group conferences, as in Australia and New Zealand, or police cautioning schemes, or sentencing circles; it can overlap with mediation between victim and offender. There is nothing restorative justice can achieve if the perpetrator does not accept some responsibility, does not admit that he or she is guilty and does not repent. In many parts of the world, restorative justice is prohibited from being used for crimes against women. Increasing use in cases of intimate violence has created deep concerns among feminist anti-violence activists, especially because very little research supports its use in such cases.

Though the rapist may believe that he has ruined his victim's life, this will not be true unless the victim believes it to be so. What cannot be denied is that the convicted rapist has ruined his own life. All too often the rapist has a history of having been sexually abused, which has taught him a version of sexual response that is callous, destructive and cruel. Restorative justice also depends upon a commonly held concept of community and the perpetrator's acceptance of the idea of membership of it. A perpetrator who considers himself a marauding outcast is not likely to care whether his victim's community forgives him or understands him.

Amid the insoluble inconsistencies in the law of rape one thing is becoming clear. Women are claiming the right to denounce their assailant. In a criminal trial they don't get to tell their story in a coherent or connected fashion, nor do they get the chance to demonstrate to the perpetrator how he has wronged them. Rape survivor Emma Riggs explained where she stood, 'Restorative justice is not for everyone but, for me, knowing I've faced my rapist head-on and emerged on the other side stronger makes me feel I can achieve anything.'[26] After her interview with the prosecutor, Gretchen Casey, another survivor, decided that she would never, ever talk about her rape again. 'My life is going forward,' she said, 'I am not stuck on that day.'[27] Joanne Nodding too was put out when the judge told her assailant that he had 'destroyed her life'. 'That wasn't what I wanted and that wasn't how I saw it,' she explained.[28] Emily McCombs didn't wait for a mediator to arrange a meeting with one of the men who assaulted her when she was fourteen.

I actually called him up on the phone and talked to him about the details of my assault, those same details that had been subject to so much scrutiny. It was a crazy thing to do, and he could have denied everything, but luckily for my mental health, he didn't.

Instead, he said something to me that turned out to be an absolute gift: 'You're not crazy. I was there. I remember. It happened.' In verifying my memories, he restored something in me that had been eroded by doubt. He reminded me that I was telling the truth, that I was to be believed.[29]

McCombs took a risk but in taking it she managed to take control of her situation. Hannah Orenstein too came to the conclusion that she had to speak up about what had happened to her.

For six months after I was raped, I didn't think I would ever write again—not about the incident, and not about anything else. I thought that the person I had been *before* the assault and the person I was afterward were different.

And I was right. I *did* change. I took control of my narrative.[30]

Is there a way forward through the reality of sexual violence? It seems that heterosex is in serious trouble. At all points in the life career, males and females make a bad fit. Young women embark on relationships with young men whom they dare not even ask to use a condom. Many will have been vaccinated against human papillomavirus (HPV) when they were too young to engage in penetrative sex. Their focus is all on keeping their partner and that means keeping him happy.

Women in search of romance are coming to grief at the hands of men who are after conquest. When they meet with casual brutality they are deeply humiliated and traumatised. If they look for redress they will certainly be further harassed and intruded upon, and their cause is all too likely to fail, leaving them further injured and demoralised.

The figures we have about the prevalence of rape and its effects are too soft to be called statistics. The media concern themselves with spectacular cases which they report in soul-crushing detail; one way of mitigating the victim's pain could be to do as has been done in the Republic of Ireland, which is to hear such cases in a closed court. The Republic also provides a statutory definition of consent and is considering adopting something like the system used in France and Belgium where the complainant has representation and is a party in the case. One aspect of a rape trial that never ceases to amaze is that a complex of offences will be cleared as if they were a single offence, as happened in the recent trial of four rugby players in Belfast who, despite clear evidence of revoltingly brutal behaviour, were cleared of all charges. One approach could be to separate the elements of assault for which consent is not an issue from the actual rape in which it is the only issue. It should be possible then to convict on the assault charges while leaving the rape issue moot.

My concern is however larger. If non-consensual sex is, as seems obvious to me, commoner than deep communion between male and female, we must make an attempt to stem its deadening spread. But how? Sexual culture is protean; it changes constantly, in response to myriad prompts from the cultural environment. In this essay I have made no mention of pornography, or of the consequences of beginning sexual behaviour as solitary masturbation and only later, sometimes much later, involving another person. Once upon a time we talked about making love, almost as if we realised that love is a project requiring mutual creativity and cooperation. What builds it is not the presence of an organ in a body orifice, but what enters the mind, never to be forgotten, the words spoken not the things done. Sexual imagery is everywhere, but erotic imagery is not. Perhaps we need to have less sex but better, and not at the end of a stressful working day or with the aid of too much alcohol. Men and women can between them create ecstasy if they invest time, energy and creativity in their lovemaking. Routine sex shades too easily into mere sufferance. In such cases, in the words of John Donne's poem 'The Extasie', 'A great Prince in prison lies'.

Heterosex may well be doomed. For women, who are viscerally attached to the sons they have borne, and to the men they have loved, and to their fathers, a same-sex no-sex world may well turn out to be an impoverished alternative. If we women love men, and we surely do, rather more I would say than they love us, we will have to find a way out of the slough of bitterness and recrimination into which we seem to have fallen.

Notes

1   Rape, Abuse and Incest National Network press release, Scott Berkowitz and Rebecca O'Connor, 2014.

2   John E B Myers, *Myers on Evidence in Child Domestic and Elder Abuse Cases*, New York NY, Aspen, 2005.

3   Margaret Sanger, *Woman and the New Race*, Truth Publishing, 1920, p. 178.

4   Bertrand Russell, *Marriage and Morals*, 1929, p. 143.

5   Alix Kates Shulman, 'Sex and Power: Sexual Bases of Radical Feminism', *Signs*, 5:4, Summer, 1980.

6   'The American Survey', *ABC News*, 2004.

7   Diana Appleyard, 'The Big O-No', *The Sun*, 18 April 2017.

8   George Galloway, 'Good night with George Galloway' podcast, 19 August 2012.

9   Per Samuelsson, Swedish Radio, 19 May 2017.

10   Bianca Fileborn, 'Sexual Assault Laws in Australia', Australian Institute of Family Studies, February 2011.

11   Hiram Kümper, 'Learned Men and Skilful Matrons: Medical Expertise and the Forensics of Rape in the Middle Ages' in Wendy J Turner and Sara M Butler, eds, *Medicine and the Law in the Middle Ages*, Leiden Brill, 2014.

12   Laura C Wilson and K E Miller, 'Meta-Analysis of the prevalence of Unacknowledged Rape', *Trauma, Violence, Abuse*, Epub, 17 March 2015.

13   Gabrielle Union, *We're Going to Need More Wine*, HarperCollins Publishers, New York, 2017.

14   Moira Donovan, 'I started the Media Men List My name is Moira Donovan', *New York Magazine*, 10 January 1918.

15   Wade Institute eNewsletter, 30 October 2017.

16   Janice Zoucha-Jensen and Anne Coyne, 'The Effects of Resistance Strategies on Rape,' *American Journal of Public Health*, 83:11, 1993.

17   *The Guardian*, 21 March 2018.